Miscellaneous Poems by George Crabbe

George Crabbe was born on December 24th, 1754 in Aldeburgh, Suffolk. He was sent to school at a very young age and soon developed an avid and precocious interest in books.

Crabbe was sent first to a boarding-school at Bungay, and a few years later to a school at Stowmarket, where he learnt mathematics and Latin. His early reading included William Shakespeare, Alexander Pope, Abraham Cowley, Sir Walter Raleigh and Edmund Spenser.

Medicine had now been settled on as his future career and, after three years at Stowmarket, in 1768, he was apprenticed to a local doctor at Wickhambrook, near Bury St Edmunds.

In 1772, a lady's magazine offered a prize for the best poem on 'hope'. Crabbe entered and won. The magazine then printed other short pieces of his during the year.

His first major work, Inebriety, was self-published in 1775. By this time he had completed his medical training and returned to Aldeburgh. Low finances meant his intention to go to London to study at a hospital was abandoned and instead he worked as a warehouseman.

The following year, 1777, he did travel to London to practice medicine, but returned home with financial woes. Crabbe continued to practice as a surgeon but with limited surgical skills, he received only the poorest of patients, together with small and undependable fees.

He moved to London again in April 1780, to see if he could make it as a poet, or, if that failed, as a doctor. By the end of May he had been forced to pawn his surgical instruments.

With the publication in May 1783 of his poem The Village, Crabbe achieved popularity with both the public and critics. Samuel Johnson said of it in a letter to Reynolds "I have sent you back Mr. Crabbe's poem, which I read with great delight. It is original, vigorous, and elegant."

In 1796 their third son, Edmund, died at the age of six. The death shredded Sarah's mental health and she never recovered. Crabbe, a devoted husband, tended her until her death many years later.

In September 1807, Crabbe published a new volume of poems which included The Library, The Newspaper, The Village and The Parish Register, to which were added Sir Eustace Grey and The Hall of Justice. It had been decades since his last publication but now he was seen as an important poet.

Crabbe's next volume of poetry, Tales, was published in 1812. It received a warm welcome from the poet's admirers, and critics. It is now considered Crabbe's masterpiece.

In the summer of 1813, Sarah felt well enough to visit London again. George, Sarah and their two sons spent nearly three months there. The family returned to Muston in September, and at October's end Sarah died at age 63.

In June 1819, Crabbe published his collection Tales of the Hall.

Around 1820 Crabbe began suffering from frequent severe attacks of neuralgia, and this, together with his age, made him less able to travel to London.

In November 1822 he went to see his son George. He was able to preach twice for his son, who congratulated him on the power of his voice. "I will venture a good sum, sir," he said, "that you will be assisting me ten years hence." "Ten weeks" was Crabbe's answer. The prediction proved eerily accurate.

George Crabbe died on February 3rd, 1832, aged 77 at Trowbridge, Wiltshire with his two sons by his side.

Index of Contents

Sir Eustace Grey
The Hall of Justice
Woman
The Birth of Flattery
Reflections
Footnotes
George Crabbe – A Short Biography
George Crabbe – A Concise Bibliography

"SIR EUSTACE GREY"

SCENE: —A MADHOUSE.

PERSONS: —VISITOR, PHYSICIAN, AND PATIENT.

"Veris miscens falsa."
SENECA.

VISITOR
I'll know no more;—the heart is torn
By views of woe we cannot heal;
Long shall I see these things forlorn,
And oft again their griefs shall feel,
As each upon the mind shall steal;
That wan projector's mystic style,
That lumpish idiot leering by,
That peevish idler's ceaseless wile,
And that poor maiden's half-form'd smile,
While struggling for the full-drawn sigh!—
I'll know no more.

PHYSICIAN

Yes, turn again;
Then speed to happier scenes thy way,
When thou hast view'd, what yet remain,
The ruins of Sir Eustace Grey,
The sport of madness, misery's prey:
But he will no historian need,
His cares, his crimes, will he display,
And show (as one from frenzy freed)
The proud lost mind, the rash-done deed.

That cell to him is Greyling Hall:—
Approach; he'll bid thee welcome there;
Will sometimes for his servant call,
And sometimes point the vacant chair:
He can, with free and easy air,
Appear attentive and polite;
Can veil his woes in manners fair,
And pity with respect excite.

PATIENT
Who comes?—Approach!—'tis kindly done:—
My learn'd physician, and a friend,
Their pleasures quit, to visit one
Who cannot to their ease attend,
Nor joys bestow, nor comforts lend,
As when I lived so blest, so well,
And dreamt not I must soon contend
With those malignant powers of hell.

PHYSICIAN
"Less warmth, Sir Eustace, or we go."

PATIENT
See! I am calm as infant love,
A very child, but one of woe,
Whom you should pity, not reprove:—
But men at ease, who never strove
With passions wild, will calmly show
How soon we may their ills remove,
And masters of their madness grow.

Some twenty years, I think, are gone,—
(Time flies I know not how, away,)
The sun upon no happier shone,
Nor prouder man, than Eustace Grey.
Ask where you would, and all would say,
The man admired and praised of all,
By rich and poor, by grave and gay,

Was the young lord of Greyling Hall.

Yes! I had youth and rosy health;
Was nobly form'd, as man might be;
For sickness, then, of all my wealth,
I never gave a single fee:
The ladies fair, the maidens free,
Were all accustom'd then to say,
Who would a handsome figure see
Should look upon Sir Eustace Grey.

He had a frank and pleasant look,
A cheerful eye and accent bland;
His very speech and manner spoke
The generous heart, the open hand;
About him all was gay or grand,
He had the praise of great and small;
He bought, improved, projected, plann'd,
And reign'd a prince at Greyling Hall.

My lady!—she was all we love;
All praise (to speak her worth) is faint;
Her manners show'd the yielding dove,
Her morals, the seraphic saint:
She never breath'd nor look'd complaint;
No equal upon earth had she—
Now, what is this fair thing I paint?
Alas! as all that live shall be.

There was, beside, a gallant youth,
And him my bosom's friend I had;—
Oh! I was rich in very truth,
It made me proud—it made me mad!—
Yes, I was lost—but there was cause!—
Where stood my tale?—I cannot find—
But I had all mankind's applause,
And all the smiles of womankind.

There were two cherub-things beside,
A gracious girl, a glorious boy;
Yet more to swell my full-blown pride,
To varnish higher my fading joy,
Pleasures were ours without alloy,
Nay, Paradise,—till my frail Eve
Our bliss was tempted to destroy—
Deceived and fated to deceive.

But I deserved;—for all that time,

When I was loved, admired, caress'd,.
There was within, each secret crime,
Unfelt, uncancell'd, unconfess'd:
I never then my God address'd,
In grateful praise or humble prayer;
And if His Word was not my jest—
(Dread thought!) it never was my care.

I doubted: —fool I was to doubt!
If that all-piercing eye could see,—
If He who looks all worlds throughout,
Would so minute and careful be
As to perceive and punish me:—
With man I would be great and high,
But with my God so lost, that He,
In His large view should pass me by.

Thus blest with children, friend, and wife,
Blest far beyond the vulgar lot;
Of all that gladdens human life,
Where was the good that I had not?
But my vile heart had sinful spot,
And Heaven beheld its deep'ning stain;
Eternal justice I forgot,
And mercy sought not to obtain.

Come near,—I'll softly speak the rest!—
Alas! 'tis known to all the crowd,
Her guilty love was all confess'd;
And his, who so much truth avow'd,
My faithless friend's.—In pleasure proud
I sat, when these cursed tidings came;
Their guilt, their flight was told aloud,
And Envy smiled to hear my shame!

I call'd on Vengeance; at the word
She came: —Can I the deed forget?
I held the sword—the accursed sword
The blood of his false heart made wet;
And that fair victim paid her debt,
She pined, she died, she loath'd to live;—
I saw her dying—see her yet:
Fair fallen thing! my rage forgive!

Those cherubs still, my life to bless,
Were left; could I my fears remove,
Sad fears that check'd each fond caress,
And poison'd all parental love?

Yet that with jealous feelings strove,
And would at last have won my will,
Had I not, wretch! been doom'd to prove
Th' extremes of mortal good and ill.

In youth! health! joy! in beauty's pride!
They droop'd—as flowers when blighted bow;
The dire infection came: —they died,
And I was cursed—as I am now;—
Nay, frown not, angry friend,—allow
That I was deeply, sorely tried;
Hear then, and you must wonder how
I could such storms and strifes abide.

Storms!—not that clouds embattled make,
When they afflict this earthly globe;
But such as with their terrors shake
Man's breast, and to the bottom probe;
They make the hypocrite disrobe,
They try us all, if false or true;
For this one Devil had power on Job;
And I was long the slave of two.

PHYSICIAN
Peace, peace, my friend; these subjects fly;
Collect thy thoughts—go calmly on.—

PATIENT
And shall I then the fact deny?
I was—thou know'st—I was begone,
Like him who fill'd the eastern throne,
To whom the Watcher cried aloud;
That royal wretch of Babylon,
Who was so guilty and so proud.

Like him, with haughty, stubborn mind,
I, in my state, my comforts sought;
Delight and praise I hoped to find,
In what I builded, planted! bought!
Oh! arrogance! by misery taught—
Soon came a voice! I felt it come;
"Full be his cup, with evil fraught,
Demons his guides, and death his doom!"

Then was I cast from out my state;
Two fiends of darkness led my way;
They waked me early, watch'd me late,
My dread by night, my plague by day!

Oh! I was made their sport, their play,
Through many a stormy troubled year;
And how they used their passive prey
Is sad to tell: —but you shall hear.

And first before they sent me forth.
Through this unpitying world to run,
They robb'd Sir Eustace of his worth,
Lands, manors, lordships, every one;
So was that gracious man undone,
Was spurn'd as vile, was scorn'd as poor,
Whom every former friend would shun,
And menials drove from every door.

Then rose ill-favour'd Ones, whom none
But my unhappy eyes could view,
Led me, with wild emotion, on,
And, with resistless terror, drew.
Through lands we fled, o'er seas we flew,
And halted on a boundless plain;
Where nothing fed, nor breathed, nor grew,
But silence ruled the still domain.

Upon that boundless plain, below,
The setting sun's last rays were shed,
And gave a mild and sober glow,
Where all were still, asleep, or dead;
Vast ruins in the midst were spread,
Pillars and pediments sublime,
Where the gray mass had form'd a bed,
And clothed the crumbling spoils of time.

There was I fix'd, I know not how,
Condemn'd for untold years to stay:
Yet years were not;—one dreadful Now
Endured no change of night or day;
The same mild evening's sleeping ray
Shone softly solemn and serene,
And all that time I gazed away,
The setting sun's sad rays were seen.

At length a moment's sleep stole on,—
Again came my commission'd foes;
Again through sea and land we're gone,
No peace, no respite, no repose;
Above the dark broad sea we rose,
We ran through bleak and frozen land;
I had no strength their strength t'oppose,

An infant in a giant's hand.

They placed me where those streamers play,
Those nimble beams of brilliant light;
It would the stoutest heart dismay,
To see, to feel, that dreadful sight:
So swift, so pure, so cold, so bright,
They pierced my frame with icy wound;
And all that half-year's polar night,
Those dancing streamers wrapp'd me round.

Slowly that darkness pass'd away,
When down upon the earth I fell,—
Some hurried sleep was mine by day;
But soon as toll'd the evening bell,
They forced me on, where ever dwell
Far-distant men, in cities fair,
Cities of whom no travellers tell,
Nor feet but mine were wanderers there.

Their watchmen stare, and stand aghast,
As on we hurry through the dark;
The watch-light blinks as we go past,
The watch-dog shrinks and fears to bark;
The watch-tower's bell sounds shrill; and, hark
The free wind blows—we've left the town—
A wild sepulchral ground I mark,
And on a tombstone place me down.

What monuments of mighty dead!
What tombs of various kinds are found!
And stones erect their shadows shed
On humble graves, with wickers bound,
Some risen fresh, above the ground,
Some level with the native clay:
What sleeping millions wait the sound,
"Arise, ye dead, and come away!"

Alas! they stay not for that call;
Spare me this woe! ye demons, spare!
They come! the shrouded shadows all,—
'Tis more than mortal brain can bear;
Rustling they rise, they sternly glare
At man upheld by vital breath;
Who, led by wicked fiends, should dare
To join the shadowy troops of death!

Yes, I have felt all man can feel,

Till he shall pay his nature's debt;
Ills that no hope has strength to heal,
No mind the comfort to forget:
Whatever cares the heart can fret,
The spirits wear, the temper gall,
Woe, want, dread, anguish, all beset
My sinful soul!—together all!

Those fiends upon a shaking fen
Fix'd me, in dark tempestuous night;
There never trod the foot of men,
There flock'd the fowl in wint'ry flight;
There danced the moor's deceitful light
Above the pool where sedges grow;
And when the morning-sun shone bright,
It shone upon a field of snow.

They hung me on a bow so small,
The rook could build her nest no higher;
They fix'd me on the trembling ball
That crowns the steeple's quiv'ring spire;
They set me where the seas retire,
But drown with their returning tide;
And made me flee the mountain's fire,
When rolling from its burning side.

I've hung upon the ridgy steep
Of cliffs, and held the rambling brier;
I've plunged below the billowy deep,
Where air was sent me to respire;
I've been where hungry wolves retire;
And (to complete my woes) I've ran
Where Bedlam's crazy crew conspire
Against the life of reasoning man.

I've furl'd in storms the flapping sail,
By hanging from the topmast-head;
I've served the vilest slaves in jail,
And pick'd the dunghill's spoil for bread;
I've made the badger's hole my bed:
I've wander'd with a gipsy crew;
I've dreaded all the guilty dread,
And done what they would fear to do.

On sand, where ebbs and flows the flood,
Midway they placed and bade me die;
Propp'd on my staff, I stoutly stood
When the swift waves came rolling by;

And high they rose, and still more high,
Till my lips drank the bitter brine;
I sobb'd convulsed, then cast mine eye,
And saw the tide's re-flowing sign.

And then, my dreams were such as nought
Could yield but my unhappy case;
I've been of thousand devils caught,
And thrust into that horrid place
Where reign dismay, despair, disgrace;
Furies with iron fangs were there,
To torture that accursed race
Doom'd to dismay, disgrace, despair.

Harmless I was; yet hunted down
For treasons, to my soul unfit;
I've been pursued through many a town,
For crimes that petty knaves commit;
I've been adjudged t'have lost my wit,
Because I preached so loud and well;
And thrown into the dungeon's pit,
For trampling on the pit of hell.

Such were the evils, man of sin,
That I was fated to sustain;
And add to all, without—within,
A soul defiled with every stain
That man's reflecting mind can pain;
That pride, wrong, rage, despair, can make;
In fact, they'd nearly touch'd my brain,
And reason on her throne would shake.

But pity will the vilest seek,
If punish'd guilt will not repine,—
I heard a heavenly teacher speak,
And felt the SUN OF MERCY shine:
I hailed the light! the birth divine!
And then was seal'd among the few;
Those angry fiends beheld the sign,
And from me in an instant flew.

Come hear how thus the charmers cry
To wandering sheep, the strays of sin,
While some the wicket-gate pass by,
And some will knock and enter in:
Full joyful 'tis a soul to win,
For he that winneth souls is wise;
Now hark! the holy strains begin,

And thus the sainted preacher cries: —[1]

"Pilgrim, burthen'd with thy sin,
Come the way to Zion's gate,
There, till Mercy let thee in,
Knock and weep and watch and wait.
Knock!—He knows the sinner's cry!
Weep!—He loves the mourner's tears:
Watch!—for saving grace is nigh:
Wait,—till heavenly light appears.

"Hark! it is the Bridegroom's voice:
Welcome, pilgrim, to thy rest;
Now within the gate rejoice,
Safe and seal'd and bought and blest!
Safe—from all the lures of vice,
Seal'd—by signs the chosen know,
Bought—by love and life the price,
Blest—the mighty debt to owe.

"Holy Pilgrim! what for thee
In a world like this remain?
From thy guarded breast shall flee
Fear and shame, and doubt and pain.
Fear—the hope of Heaven shall fly,
Shame—from glory's view retire,
Doubt—in certain rapture die,
Pain—in endless bliss expire."

But though my day of grace was come,
Yet still my days of grief I find;
The former clouds' collected gloom
Still sadden the reflecting mind;
The soul, to evil things consign'd,
Will of their evil some retain;
The man will seem to earth inclined,
And will not look erect again.

Thus, though elect, I feel it hard
To lose what I possess'd before,
To be from all my wealth debarr'd,—
The brave Sir Eustace is no more:
But old I wax, and passing poor,
Stern, rugged men my conduct view;
They chide my wish, they bar my door,
'Tis hard—I weep—you see I do.—

Must you, my friends, no longer stay?

Thus quickly all my pleasures end;
But I'll remember when I pray,
My kind physician and his friend;
And those sad hours, you deign to spend
With me, I shall requite them all;
Sir Eustace for his friends shall send,
And thank their love at Greyling Hall.

VISITOR

The poor Sir Eustace!—Yet his hope
Leads him to think of joys again;
And when his earthly visions droop,
His views of heavenly kind remain:
But whence that meek and humbled strain,
That spirit wounded, lost, resign'd?
Would not so proud a soul disdain
The madness of the poorest mind?

PHYSICIAN

No! for the more he swell'd with pride,
The more he felt misfortune's blow;
Disgrace and grief he could not hide,
And poverty had laid him low:
Thus shame and sorrow working slow,
At length this humble spirit gave;
Madness on these began to grow,
And bound him to his fiends a slave.

Though the wild thoughts had touch'd his brain,
Then was he free: —So, forth he ran;
To soothe or threat, alike were vain:
He spake of fiends; look'd wild and wan;
Year after year, the hurried man
Obey'd those fiends from place to place;
Till his religious change began
To form a frenzied child of grace.

For, as the fury lost its strength,
The mind reposed; by slow degrees
Came lingering hope, and brought at length,
To the tormented spirit, ease:
This slave of sin, whom fiends could seize,
Felt or believed their power had end:—
"'Tis faith," he cried, "my bosom frees,
And now my SAVIOUR is my friend."

But ah! though time can yield relief,
And soften woes it cannot cure;

Would we not suffer pain and grief,
To have our reason sound and sure?
Then let us keep our bosoms pure,
Our fancy's favourite flights suppress;
Prepare the body to endure,
And bend the mind to meet distress;
And then HIS guardian care implore,
Whom demons dread and men adore.

"THE HALL OF JUSTICE", IN TWO PARTS

PART I

Confiteor facere hoc annos; sed et altera causa est,
Anxietas animi, continuusque dolor.
OVID.

MAGISTRATE, VAGRANT, CONSTABLE, &c.

VAGRANT
Take, take away thy barbarous hand,
And let me to thy Master speak;
Remit awhile the harsh command,
And hear me, or my heart will break.

MAGISTRATE
Fond wretch! and what canst thou relate,
But deeds of sorrow, shame, and sin?
Thy crime is proved, thou know'st thy fate;
But come, thy tale!—begin, begin!—

VAGRANT
My crime!—This sick'ning child to feed.
I seized the food, your witness saw;
I knew your laws forbade the deed,
But yielded to a stronger law.

Know'st thou, to Nature's great command
All human laws are frail and weak?
Nay! frown not—stay his eager hand,
And hear me, or my heart will break.

In this, th' adopted babe I hold
With anxious fondness to my breast,
My heart's sole comfort I behold,

More dear than life, when life was blest;
I saw her pining, fainting, cold,
I begg'd—but vain was my request.

I saw the tempting food, and seized—
My infant-sufferer found relief;
And in the pilfer'd treasure pleased,
Smiled on my guilt, and hush'd my grief.

But I have griefs of other kind,
Troubles and sorrows more severe;
Give me to ease my tortured mind,
Lend to my woes a patient ear;
And let me—if I may not find
A friend to help—find one to hear.

Yet nameless let me plead—my name
Would only wake the cry of scorn;
A child of sin, conceived in shame,
Brought forth in woe, to misery born.

My mother dead, my father lost,
I wander'd with a vagrant crew;
A common care, a common cost;
Their sorrows and their sins I knew;
With them, by want on error forced,
Like them, I base and guilty grew.

Few are my years, not so my crimes;
The age which these sad looks declare,
Is Sorrow's work, it is not Time's,
And I am old in shame and care.

Taught to believe the world a place
Where every stranger was a foe,
Train'd in the arts that mark our race,
To what new people could I go?
Could I a better life embrace,
Or live as virtue dictates? No!—

So through the land I wandering went,
And little found of grief or joy;
But lost my bosom's sweet content
When first I loved the Gipsy-Boy.

A sturdy youth he was and tall,
His looks would all his soul declare;
His piercing eyes were deep and small,

And strongly curl'd his raven-hair.

Yes, AARON had each manly charm,
All in the May of youthful pride,
He scarcely fear'd his father's arm,
And every other arm defied.—

Oft, when they grew in anger warm,
(Whom will not love and power divide?)
I rose, their wrathful souls to calm,
Not yet in sinful combat tried.

His father was our party's chief,
And dark and dreadful was his look;
His presence fill'd my heart with grief,
Although to me he kindly spoke.

With Aaron I delighted went,
His favour was my bliss and pride;
In growing hope our days we spent,
Love's growing charms in either spied;
It saw them all which Nature lent,
It lent them all which she denied.

Could I the father's kindness prize,
Or grateful looks on him bestow,
Whom I beheld in wrath arise,
When Aaron sunk beneath his blow?

He drove him down with wicked hand,
It was a dreadful sight to see;
Then vex'd him, till he left the land,
And told his cruel love to me;
The clan were all at his command,
Whatever his command might be.

The night was dark, the lanes were deep,
And one by one they took their way;
He bade me lay me down and sleep,
I only wept and wish'd for day.

Accursed be the love he bore,
Accursed was the force he used,
So let him of his God implore
For mercy, and be so refused!

You frown again,—to show my wrong
Can I in gentle language speak?

My woes are deep, my words are strong,—
And hear me, or my heart will break.

MAGISTRATE
I hear thy words, I feel thy pain;
Forbear awhile to speak thy woes;
Receive our aid, and then again
The story of thy life disclose.

For, though seduced and led astray,
Thou'st travell'd far and wander'd long;
Thy God hath seen thee all the way,
And all the turns that led thee wrong.

PART II

Quondam ridentes oculi, nunc fonte perenni
Deplorant poenas nocte dieque suas.
CORNEILLE.

MAGISTRATE
Come, now again thy woes impart,
Tell all thy sorrows, all thy sin;
We cannot heal the throbbing heart
Till we discern the wounds within.

Compunction weeps our guilt away,
The sinner's safety is his pain;
Such pangs for our offences pay,
And these severer griefs are gain.

VAGRANT
The son came back—he found us wed,
Then dreadful was the oath he swore;
His way through Blackburn Forest led,—
His father we beheld no more.

Of all our daring clan not one
Would on the doubtful subject dwell;
For all esteem'd the injured son,
And fear'd the tale which he could tell.

But I had mightier cause for fear,
For slow and mournful round my bed
I saw a dreadful form appear,—
It came when I and Aaron wed.

Yes! we were wed, I know my crime,—
We slept beneath the elmin tree;
But I was grieving all the time,
And Aaron frown'd my tears to see.

For he not yet had felt the pain
That rankles in a wounded breast;
He waked to sin, then slept again,
Forsook his God, yet took his rest.

But I was forced to feign delight,
And joy in mirth and music sought,—
And mem'ry now recalls the night,
With such surprise and horror fraught,

That reason felt a moment's flight,
And left a mind to madness wrought.
When waking, on my heaving breast
I felt a hand as cold as death:

A sudden fear my voice suppress'd,
A chilling terror stopp'd my breath.
I seem'd—no words can utter how!
For there my father-husband stood,

And thus he said: —"Will God allow,
The great Avenger just and Good,
A wife to break her marriage vow?
A son to shed his father's blood?"

I trembled at the dismal sounds,
But vainly strove a word to say;
So, pointing to his bleeding wounds,
The threat'ning spectre stalk'd away.

I brought a lovely daughter forth,
His father's child, in Aaron's bed;
He took her from me in his wrath,
"Where is my child?"—"Thy child is dead."

'Twas false—we wander'd far and wide,
Through town and country, field and fen,
Till Aaron, fighting, fell and died,
And I became a wife again.

I then was young: —my husband sold
My fancied charms for wicked price;

He gave me oft for sinful gold,
The slave, but not the friend of vice: —

Behold me, Heaven! my pains behold,
And let them for my sins suffice.
The wretch who lent me thus for gain,
Despised me when my youth was fled;

Then came disease, and brought me pain:—
Come, Death, and bear me to the dead!
For though I grieve, my grief is vain,
And fruitless all the tears I shed.

True, I was not to virtue train'd,
Yet well I knew my deeds were ill;
By each offence my heart was pain'd
I wept, but I offended still;

My better thoughts my life disdain'd,
But yet the viler led my will.
My husband died, and now no more
My smile was sought, or ask'd my hand,

A widow'd vagrant, vile and poor,
Beneath a vagrant's vile command.
Ceaseless I roved the country round,
To win my bread by fraudful arts,

And long a poor subsistence found,
By spreading nets for simple hearts.
Though poor, and abject, and despised,
Their fortunes to the crowd I told;

I gave the young the love they prized,
And promised wealth to bless the old.
Schemes for the doubtful I devised,
And charms for the forsaken sold.

At length for arts like these confined
In prison with a lawless crew,
I soon perceived a kindred mind,
And there my long-lost daughter knew;

His father's child, whom Aaron gave
To wander with a distant clan,
The miseries of the world to brave,
And be the slave of vice and man.

She knew my name—we met in pain;
Our parting pangs can I express?
She sail'd a convict o'er the main,
And left an heir to her distress.

This is that heir to shame and pain,
For whom I only could descry
A world of trouble and disdain:
Yet, could I bear to see her die,
Or stretch her feeble hands in vain,
And, weeping, beg of me supply?

No! though the fate thy mother knew
Was shameful! shameful though thy race
Have wander'd all a lawless crew,
Outcasts despised in every place;

Yet as the dark and muddy tide,
When far from its polluted source,
Becomes more pure and purified,
Flows in a clear and happy course;

In thee, dear infant! so may end
Our shame, in thee our sorrows cease,
And thy pure course will then extend,
In floods of joy, o'er vales of peace.

Oh! by the GOD who loves to spare,
Deny me not the boon I crave;
Let this loved child your mercy share,
And let me find a peaceful grave:

Make her yet spotless soul your care,
And let my sins their portion have;
Her for a better fate prepare,
And punish whom 'twere sin to save!

MAGISTRATE
Recall the word, renounce the thought,
Command thy heart and bend thy knee;
There is to all a pardon brought,
A ransom rich, assured and free;
'Tis full when found, 'tis found if sought,
Oh! seek it, till 'tis seal'd to thee.

VAGRANT
But how my pardon shall I know?

MAGISTRATE

By feeling dread that 'tis not sent,
By tears for sin that freely flow,
By grief, that all thy tears are spent,
By thoughts on that great debt we owe,
With all the mercy God has lent,
By suffering what thou canst not show,
Yet showing how thine heart is rent,
Till thou canst feel thy bosom glow,
And say, "MY SAVIOUR, I REPENT!"

1807

"WOMAN!"

To a Woman I never addressed myself in the language of decency and friendship, without receiving a decent and friendly answer. If I was hungry or thirsty, wet or sick, they did not hesitate, like Men, to perform a generous action: in so free and kind a manner did they contribute to my relief, that if I was dry, I drank the sweetest draught, and if hungry, I ate the coarsest morsel with a double relish.

Mr Ledyard, as quoted by Mungo Park in his travels into Africa.

Place the white man on Afric's coast,
Whose swarthy sons in blood delight,
Who of their scorn to Europe boast,
And paint their very demons white:
There, while the sterner sex disdains
To soothe the woes they cannot feel,
Woman will strive to heal his pains,
And weep for those she cannot heal:
Hers is warm pity's sacred glow;
From all her stores she bears a part,
And bids the spring of hope re-flow,
That languish'd in the fainting heart.

"What though so pale his haggard face,
So sunk and sad his looks,"—she cries;
"And far unlike our nobler race,
With crisped locks and rolling eyes;
Yet misery marks him of our kind;
We see him lost, alone, afraid;
And pangs of body, griefs in mind,
Pronounce him man, and ask our aid.

"Perhaps in some far-distant shore
There are who in these forms delight;

Whose milky features please them more,
Than ours of jet thus burnished bright;
Of such may be his weeping wife,
Such children for their sire may call,
And if we spare his ebbing life,
Our kindness may preserve them all."

Thus her compassion Woman shows:
Beneath the line her acts are these;
Nor the wide waste of Lapland-snows
Can her warm flow of pity freeze:—
"From some sad land the stranger comes,
Where joys like ours are never found;
Let's soothe him in our happy homes,
Where freedom sits, with plenty crown'd.

'Tis good the fainting soul to cheer,
To see the famish'd stranger fed;
To milk for him the mother-deer,
To smooth for him the furry bed.
The powers above our Lapland bless
With good no other people know;
T'enlarge the joys that we possess,
By feeling those that we bestow!"

Thus in extremes of cold and heat,
Where wandering man may trace his kind;
Wherever grief and want retreat,
In Woman they compassion find;
She makes the female breast her seat,
And dictates mercy to the mind.

Man may the sterner virtues know,
Determined justice, truth severe;
But female hearts with pity glow,
And Woman holds affliction dear;
For guiltless woes her sorrows flow,
And suffering vice compels her tear;
'Tis hers to soothe the ills below,
And bid life's fairer views appear:
To Woman's gentle kind we owe
What comforts and delights us here;
They its gay hopes on youth bestow,
And care they soothe, and age they cheer.

1807

"THE BIRTH OF FLATTERY"

Omnia habeo, nec quicquam habeo;
Quidquid, dicunt, laudo; id rursum si negant, laudo id quoque;
Negat quis, nego; ait, aio;
Postremo imperavi egomet mihi
Omnia assentari.
TERENCE, *in Eunuch.*

'Tis an old maxim in the schools,
That flattery is the food of fools;
Yet now and then your men of wit
Will condescend to taste a bit.
SWIFT.

The Subiect—Poverty and Cunning described—When united, a jarring Couple—Mutual reproof—the Wife consoled by a Dream—Birth of a Daughter—Description and Prediction of Envy—How to be rendered ineffectual, explained in a Vision—Simulation foretells the future Success and Triumphs of Flattery—Her power over various Characters and Different Minds; over certain Classes of Men; over Envy himself—Her successful Art of softening the Evils of Life; of changing Characters; of meliorating Prospects and affixing Value to Possessions, Pictures, &c. Conclusion.

Muse of my Spenser, who so well could sing
The passions all, their bearings and their ties;
Who could in view those shadowy beings bring,
And with bold hand remove each dark disguise,
Wherein love, hatred, scorn, or anger lies:
Guide him to Fairy-land, who now intends
That way his flight; assist him as he flies,
To mark those passions, Virtue's foes and friends,
By whom when led she droops, when leading she ascends.
Yes! they appear, I see the fairy train!
And who that modest nymph of meek address?
Not vanity, though loved by all the vain;
Not Hope, though promising to all success;
Not Mirth, nor Joy, though foe to all distress;
Thee, sprightly syren, from this train I choose,
Thy birth relate, thy soothing arts confess;
'Tis not in thy mild nature to refuse,
When poets ask thine aid, so oft their meed and muse.

In Fairy-land, on wide and cheerless plain,
Dwelt, in the house of Care a sturdy swain;
A hireling he, who, when he till'd the soil,
Look'd to the pittance that repaid his toil,
And to a master left the mingled joy
And anxious care that follow'd his employ.

Sullen and patient he at once appear'd,
As one who murmur'd, yet as one who fear'd;
Th'attire was coarse that clothed his sinewy frame,
Rude his address, and Poverty his name.
In that same plain a nymph, of curious taste,
A cottage (plann'd, with all her skill) had placed;
Strange the materials, and for what design'd
The various parts, no simple man might find;
What seem'd the door, each entering guest withstood,
What seem'd a window was but painted wood;
But by a secret spring the wall would move,
And daylight drop through glassy door above:
'Twas all her pride, new traps for praise to lay,
And all her wisdom was to hide her way;
In small attempts incessant were her pains,
And Cunning was her name among the swains.
Now, whether fate decreed this pair should wed,
And blindly drove them to the marriage bed;
Or whether love in some soft hour inclined
The damsel's heart, and won her to be kind,
Is yet unsung: they were an ill-match'd pair,
But both disposed to wed—and wed they were.
Yet, though united in their fortune, still
Their ways were diverse; varying was their will;
Nor long the maid had bless'd the simple man,
Before dissensions rose, and she began:—
"Wretch that I am! since to thy fortune bound,
What plan, what project, with success is crown'd?
I, who a thousand secret arts possess,
Who every rank approach with right address;
Who've loosed a guinea from a miser's chest,
And worm'd his secret from a traitor's breast;
Thence gifts and gains collecting, great and small,
Have brought to thee, and thou consum'st them all;
For want like thine—a bog without a base—
Ingulfs all gains I gather for the place;
Feeding, unfill'd; destroying, undestroy'd;
It craves for ever, and is ever void:—
Wretch that I am! what misery have I found,
Since my sure craft was to thy calling bound!"
"Oh! vaunt of worthless art," the swain replied,
Scowling contempt, "how pitiful this pride!
What are these specious gifts, these paltry gains,
But base rewards for ignominious pains?
With all thy tricking, still for bread we strive,
Thine is, proud wretch! the care that cannot thrive;
By all thy boasted skill and baffled hooks,
Thou gain'st no more than students by their books.

No more than I for my poor deeds am paid,
Whom none can blame, will help, or dare upbraid.
"Call this our need, a bog that all devours,—
Then what thy petty arts, but summer-flowers,
Gaudy and mean, and serving to betray
The place they make unprofitably gay?
Who know it not, some useless beauties see,—
But ah! to prove it was reserved for me."
Unhappy state! that, in decay of love,
Permits harsh truth his errors to disprove;
While he remains, to wrangle and to jar,
Is friendly tournament, not fatal war;
Love in his play will borrow arms of hate,
Anger and rage, upbraiding and debate;
And by his power the desperate weapons thrown,
Become as safe and pleasant as his own;
But left by him, their natures they assume,
And fatal, in their poisoning force, become.
Time fled, and now the swain compell'd to see
New cause for fear—"Is this thy thrift?" quoth he,
To whom the wife with cheerful voice replied:—
"Thou moody man, lay all thy fears aside;
I've seen a vision—they, from whom I came,
A daughter promise, promise wealth and fame;
Born with my features, with my arts, yet she
Shall patient, pliant, persevering be,
And in thy better ways resemble thee.
The fairies round shall at her birth attend,
The friend of all in all shall find a friend,
And save that one sad star that hour must gleam
On our fair child, how glorious were my dream?"
This heard the husband, and, in surly smile,
Aim'd at contempt, but yet he hoped the while;
For as, when sinking, wretched men are found
To catch at rushes rather than be drown'd;
So on a dream our peasant placed his hope,
And found that rush as valid as a rope.
Swift fled the days, for now in hope they fled,
When a fair daughter bless'd the nuptial bed;
Her infant-face the mother's pains beguiled,
She look'd so pleasing and so softly smiled;
Those smiles, those looks, with sweet sensations moved
The gazer's soul, and as he look'd he loved.
And now the fairies came with gifts, to grace
So mild a nature, and so fair a face.
They gave, with beauty, that bewitching art,
That holds in easy chains the human heart;
They gave her skill to win the stubborn mind,

To make the suffering to their sorrows blind,
To bring on pensive looks the pleasing smile,
And Care's stern brow of every frown beguile.
These magic favours graced the infant-maid,
Whose more enlivening smile the charming gifts repaid.
Now Fortune changed, who, were she constant long,
Would leave us few adventures for our song.
A wicked elfin roved this land around,
Whose joys proceeded from the griefs he found;
Envy his name: —his fascinating eye
From the light bosom drew the sudden sigh;
Unsocial he, but with malignant mind,
He dwelt with man, that he might curse mankind;
Like the first foe, he sought th' abode of Joy
Grieved to behold, but eager to destroy;
Round blooming beauty, like the wasp, he flew,
Soil'd the fresh sweet, and changed the rosy hue;
The wise, the good, with anxious heart he saw,
And here a failing found, and there a flaw;
Discord in families 'twas his to move,
Distrust in friendship, jealousy in love;
He told the poor, what joys the great possess'd;
The great, what calm content the cottage bless'd:
To part the learned and the rich he tried,
Till their slow friendship perish'd in their pride.
Such was the fiend, and so secure of prey,
That only Misery pass'd unstung away.
Soon as he heard the fairy-babe was born,
Scornful he smiled, but felt no more than scorn:
For why, when Fortune placed her state so low,
In useless spite his lofty malice show?
Why, in a mischief of the meaner kind,
Exhaust the vigour of a ranc'rous mind;
But, soon as Fame the fairy-gifts proclaim'd,
Quick-rising wrath his ready soul inflamed
To swear, by vows that e'en the wicked tie,
The nymph should weep her varied destiny;
That every gift, that now appear'd to shine
In her fair face, and make her smiles divine,
Should all the poison of his magic prove,
And they should scorn her, whom she sought for love.
His spell prepared, in form an ancient dame,
A fiend in spirit, to the cot he came;
There gain'd admittance, and the infant press'd
(Muttering his wicked magic) to his breast;
And thus he said: —"Of all the powers who wait
On Jove's decrees, and do the work of fate,
Was I, alone, despised or worthless, found,

Weak to protect, or impotent to wound?
See then thy foe, regret the friendship lost,
And learn my skill, but learn it at your cost.
"Know, then, O child! devote to fates severe,
The good shall hate thy name, the wise shall fear;
Wit shall deride, and no protecting friend
Thy shame shall cover, or thy name defend.
Thy gentle sex, who, more than ours, should spare
A humble foe, will greater scorn declare;
The base alone thy advocates shall be,
Or boast alliance with a wretch like thee."
He spake, and vanish'd, other prey to find,
And waste in slow disease the conquer'd mind.
Awed by the elfin's threats, and fill'd with dread
The parents wept, and sought their infant's bed;
Despair alone the father's soul possess'd;
But hope rose gently in the mother's breast;
For well she knew that neither grief nor joy
Pain'd without hope, or pleased without alloy;
And while these hopes and fears her heart divide,
A cheerful vision bade the fears subside.
She saw descending to the world below
An ancient form, with solemn pace and slow.
"Daughter, no more be sad" (the phantom cried),
"Success is seldom to the wise denied;
In idle wishes fools supinely stay,
Be there a will, and wisdom finds a way:
Why art thou grieved? Be rather glad, that he
Who hates the happy, aims his darts at thee,
But aims in vain; thy favour'd daughter lies
Serenely blest, and shall to joy arise.
For, grant that curses on her name shall wait,
(So Envy wills, and such the voice of Fate,)
Yet if that name be prudently suppress'd,
She shall be courted, favour'd, and caress'd.
"For what are names? and where agree mankind,
In those to persons or to acts assign'd?
Brave, learn'd, or wise, if some their favourites call,
Have they the titles or the praise from all?
Not so, but others will the brave disdain
As rash, and deem the sons of wisdom vain;
The self-same mind shall scorn or kindness move,
And the same deed attract contempt and love.
"So all the powers who move the human soul,
With all the passions who the will control,
Have various names—One giv'n by Truth Divine,
(As Simulation thus was fixed for mine,)
The rest by man, who now, as wisdom's prize

My secret counsels, now as art despise;
One hour, as just, those counsels they embrace,
And spurn, the next, as pitiful and base.
Thee, too, my child, those fools as Cunning fly,
Who on thy counsel and thy craft rely;
That worthy craft in others they condemn,
But 'tis their prudence, while conducting them.
"Be FLATTERY, then, thy happy infant's name,
Let Honour scorn her and let Wit defame;
Let all be true that Envy dooms, yet all,
Not on herself, but on her name, shall fall;
While she thy fortune and her own shall raise,
And decent Truth be call'd, and loved as, modest Praise.
"O happy child! the glorious day shall shine,
When every ear shall to thy speech incline,
Thy words alluring and thy voice divine:
The sullen pedant and the sprightly wit,
To hear thy soothing eloquence shall sit;
And both, abjuring Flattery, will agree
That Truth inspires, and they must honour thee.
"Envy himself shall to thy accents bend,
Force a faint smile, and sullenly attend,
When thou shalt call him Virtue's jealous friend,
Whose bosom glows with generous rage to find
How fools and knaves are flatter'd by mankind.
"The sage retired, who spends alone his days,
And flies th' obstreperous voice of public praise;
The vain, the vulgar cry,—shall gladly meet,
And bid thee welcome to his still retreat;
Much will he wonder, how thou cam'st to find
A man to glory dead, to peace consign'd.
O Fame! he'll cry (for he will call thee Fame),
From thee I fly, from thee conceal my name;
But thou shalt say, though Genius takes his night,
He leaves behind a glorious train of light,
And hides in vain: —yet prudent he that flies
The flatterer's art, and for himself is wise.
"Yes, happy child! I mark th'approaching day,
When warring natures will confess thy sway;
When thou shalt Saturn's golden reign restore,
And vice and folly shall be known no more.
"Pride shall not then in human-kind have place,
Changed by thy skill, to Dignity and Grace;
While Shame, who now betrays the inward sense
Of secret ill, shall be thy Diffidence;
Avarice shall thenceforth prudent Forecast be,
And bloody Vengeance, Magnanimity;
The lavish tongue shall honest truths impart,

The lavish hand shall show the generous heart,
And Indiscretion be, contempt of art;
Folly and Vice shall then, no longer known,
Be, this as Virtue, that as Wisdom, shown.
"Then shall the Robber, as the Hero, rise
To seize the good that churlish law denies;
Throughout the world shall rove the generous band,
And deal the gifts of Heaven from hand to hand.
In thy blest days no tyrant shall be seen,
Thy gracious king shall rule contented men;
In thy blest days shall not a rebel be,
But patriots all and well-approved of thee.
"Such powers are thine, that man by thee shall wrest
The gainful secret from the cautious breast;
Nor then, with all his care, the good retain,
But yield to thee the secret and the gain.
In vain shall much experience guard the heart
Against the charm of thy prevailing art;
Admitted once, so soothing is thy strain,
It comes the sweeter, when it comes again;
And when confess'd as thine, what mind so strong
Forbears the pleasure it indulged so long?
"Softener of every ill! of all our woes
The balmy solace! friend of fiercest foes!
Begin thy reign, and like the morning rise!
Bring joy, bring beauty, to our eager eyes;
Break on the drowsy world like opening day,
While grace and gladness join thy flow'ry way;
While every voice is praise, while every heart is gay.
"From thee all prospects shall new beauties take,
'Tis thine to seek them and 'tis thine to make;
On the cold fen I see thee turn thine eyes,
Its mists recede, its chilling vapour flies;
Th'enraptured Lord th'improving ground surveys,
And for his Eden asks the traveller's praise,
Which yet, unview'd of thee, a bog had been,
Where spungy rushes hide the plashy green.
"I see thee breathing on the barren moor,
That seems to bloom although so bleak before;
There, if beneath the gorse the primrose spring,
Or the pied daisy smile below the ling,
They shall new charms, at thy command disclose,
And none shall miss the myrtle or the rose.
The wiry moss, that whitens all the hill,
Shall live a beauty by thy matchless skill;
Gale from the bog shall yield Arabian balm,
And the gray willow give a golden palm.
"I see thee smiling in the pictured room,

Now breathing beauty, now reviving bloom;
There, each immortal name 'tis thine to give,
To graceless forms, and bid the lumber live.
Should'st thou coarse boors or gloomy martyrs see,
These shall thy Guidos, these thy Teniers be;
There shalt thou Raphael's saints and angels trace,
There make for Rubens and for Reynolds place,
And all the pride of art shall find, in her disgrace.
"Delight of either sex? thy reign commence;
With balmy sweetness soothe the weary sense,
And to the sickening soul thy cheering aid dispense.
Queen of the mind! thy golden age begin;
In mortal bosoms varnish shame and sin;
Let all be fair without, let all be calm within."
The vision fled, the happy mother rose,
Kiss'd the fair infant, smiled at all her foes,
And FLATTERY made her name: —her reign began.
Her own dear sex she ruled, then vanquished man:
A smiling friend, to every class she spoke,
Assumed their manners, and their habits took;
Her, for her humble mien, the modest loved;
Her cheerful looks the light and gay approved:
The just beheld her, firm: the valiant, brave:
Her mirth the free, her silence pleased the grave:
Zeal heard her voice, and, as he preach'd aloud,
Well pleased he caught her whispers from the crowd,
(Those whispers, soothing-sweet to every ear,
Which some refuse to pay, but none to hear):
Shame fled her presence, at her gentle strain,
Care softly smiled, and Guilt forgot its pain:
The wretched thought, the happy found, her true,
The learn'd confess'd that she her merits knew:
The rich—could they a constant friend condemn?
The poor believed—for who should flatter them?
Thus on her name though all disgrace attend,
In every creature she beholds a friend.

1807

"REFLECTIONS". UPON THE SUBJECT—

Quid juvat errores, mersa jam puppe, fateri?
Quid lacrymae delicta juvant commissa secutae?
CLAUDIAN, in Eutropium.

What avails it, when shipwreck'd, that error appears?

Are the crimes we commit wash'd away by our tears?

When all the fiercer passions cease
(The glory and disgrace of youth):
When the deluded soul in peace,
Can listen to the voice of truth:
When we are taught in whom to trust,
And how to spare, to spend, to give,
(Our prudence kind, our pity just),
'Tis then we rightly learn to live.

Its weakness when the body feels,
Nor danger in contempt defies:
To reason when desire appeals,
When, on experience, hope relies:
When every passing hour we prize,
Nor rashly on our follies spend:
But use it, as it quickly flies,
With sober aim to serious end:
When prudence bounds our utmost views,
And bids us wrath and wrong forgive:
When we can ealmly gain or lose,—
'Tis then we rightly learn to live.

Yet thus, when we our way discern,
And can upon our care depend,
To travel safely, when we learn,
Behold? we're near our journey's end.
We've trod the maze of error round,
Long wand'ring in the winding glade:
And, now the torch of truth is found,
It only shows us where we stray'd:
Light for ourselves, what is it worth,
When we no more our way can choose?
For others, when we hold it forth,
They, in their pride, the boon refuse.

By long experience taught, we now
Can rightly judge of friends and foes,
Can all the worth of these allow,
And all their faults discern in those;
Relentless hatred, erring love,
We can for sacred truth forego;
We can the warmest friend reprove,
And bear to praise the fiercest foe:
To what effect? Our friends are gone
Beyond reproof, regard, or care;
And of our foes remains there one,

The mild relenting thought to share?

Now 'tis our boast that we can quell
The wildest passions in their rage;
Can their destructive force repel,
And their impetuous wrath assuage:
Ah! Virtue, dost thou arm, when now
This bold rebellious race are fled;
When all these tyrants rest and thou
Art warring with the mighty dead?
Revenge, ambition, scorn, and pride,
And strong desire, and fierce disdain,
The giant-brood by thee defied,
Lo! Time's resistless strokes have slain.

Yet Time, who could that race subdue,
(O'erpowering strength, appeasing rage,)
Leaves yet a persevering crew,
To try the failing powers of age.
Vex'd by the constant call of these,
Virtue a while for conquest tries:
But weary grown and fond of ease,
She makes with them a compromise:
Av'rice himself she gives to rest,
But rules him with her strict commands;
Bids Pity touch his torpid breast,
And Justice hold his eager hands.

Yet is their nothing men can do,
When chilling age comes creeping on?
Cannot we yet some good pursue?
Are talents buried? genius gone?
If passions slumber in the breast,
If follies from the heart be fled;
Of laurels let us go in quest,
And place them on the poet's head.

Yes, we'll redeem the wasted time,
And to neglected studies flee;
We'll build again the lofty rhyme,
Or live, Philosophy, with thee:
For reasoning clear, for flight sublime,
Eternal fame reward shall be;
And to what glorious heights we'll climb,
The admiring crowd shall envying see.

Begin the song! begin the theme!—
Alas! and is Invention dead?

Dream we no more the golden dream?
Is Mem'ry with her treasures fled?
Yes, 'tis too late,—now Reason guides
The mind, sole judge in all debate;
And thus the important point decides,
For laurels, 'tis, alas! too late.
What is possess'd we may retain,
But for new conquests strive in vain.

Beware then, Age, that what was won,
If life's past labours, studies, views,
Be lost not, now the labour's done,
When all thy part is,—not to lose:
When thou canst toil or gain no more,
Destroy not what was gain'd before.

For, all that's gain'd of all that's good,
When time shall his weak frame destroy
(Their use then rightly understood),
Shall man, in happier state, enjoy.
Oh! argument for truth divine,
For study's cares, for virtue's strife;
To know the enjoyment will be thine,
In that renew'd, that endless life!

1807

Footnotes

[1] It has been suggested to me, that this change from restlessness to repose, in the mind of Sir Eustace, is wrought by a Methodistic call; and it is admitted to be such: a sober and rational conversion could not have happened while the disorder of the brain continued: yet the verses which follow, in a different measure, are not intended to make any religious persuasion appear ridiculous; they are to be supposed as the effect of memory in the disordered mind of the speaker, and, though evidently enthusiastic in respect to language, are not meant to convey any impropriety of sentiment.

George Crabbe – A Short Biography

George Crabbe was born on December 24th, 1754 in Aldeburgh, Suffolk, and was the eldest of six children fathered by George Crabbe Sr.

Crabbe was sent to school at a very young age and soon developed an avid and precocious interest in books. His father would often read passages from Milton and various 18th-century poets to him.

The family also subscribed to a country magazine called Martin's Philosophical Magazine. The Poet's Corner section was always given to Crabbe.

His father supported his son's interest in literature although obviously at that time thought his career would be in other areas.

Crabbe was sent first to a boarding-school at Bungay near his home, and a few years later to a more important school at Stowmarket, where he learnt mathematics and Latin, and a familiarity with the Latin classics. His early reading included the works of William Shakespeare, Alexander Pope, Abraham Cowley, Sir Walter Raleigh and Edmund Spenser.

Medicine had now been settled on as his future career and, after three years at Stowmarket, in 1768, he was apprenticed to a local doctor at Wickhambrook, near Bury St Edmunds. The doctor also kept a small farm, and Crabbe eventually spent more time doing farm labour and errands than medical work.

In 1771 he changed masters and moved to Woodbridge, here he joined a small club of young men who met at an inn for evening discussions. It was here that he also met his future wife, Sarah Elmy. Crabbe called her "Mira", and now, writing poetry, he would often refer to her as such in his poems.

In 1772, a lady's magazine offered a prize for the best poem on 'hope'. Crabbe entered and won. The magazine then printed other short pieces of his during the year.

His first major work, a satirical poem of nearly 400 lines called Inebriety, was self-published in 1775. Crabbe later said of the poem, which received little attention at the time, "Pray let not this be seen... there is very little of it that I'm not heartily ashamed of."

By this time he had completed his medical training and had returned to Aldeburgh. Low finances meant his intention to go to London to study at a hospital was abandoned and a job was taken as a warehouseman.

The following year, 1777, Crabbe did travel to London to practice medicine, but returned home with financial woes after a year. He continued to practice as a surgeon after returning, but with limited surgical skills, he received only the poorest of patients, together with small and undependable fees. This hurt his chances of an early marriage, but Sarah stayed devoted to him.

He moved to London again in April 1780, to see if he could make it as a poet, or, if that failed, as a doctor. By the end of May he had been forced to pawn his surgical instruments. But he had composed a number of works but, sadly, all failed to be published. He now wrote several letters seeking patronage, but these were also refused.

Crabbe was able to publish a poem at this time entitled The Candidate, but it was badly received by critics.

He continued to rack up debts, and was pressed by his creditors. In early 1781 he wrote a letter to Edmund Burke asking for help, in which he included samples of his poetry. Burke was swayed by Crabbe's letter and by meeting with him, giving him money to relieve his immediate wants, and assuring him that he would do all in his power to further Crabbe's literary career.

A short time later Burke told his friend Sir Joshua Reynolds that Crabbe had "the mind and feelings of a gentleman." Burke admitted Crabbe to his family circle at Beaconsfield. The time he spent with Burke and his family exposed him to further knowledge and ideas as well as new and valuable friends including Samuel Johnson. He completed his unfinished poems and revised others with the help of Burke's criticism. Burke helped him have his poem, The Library, published anonymously in June 1781, it was greeted with modest praise by critics, and some public appreciation.

Burke realised that Crabbe was more suited to be a clergyman than a surgeon. On his recommendation he was ordained to the curacy and then returned to Aldeburgh. His fellow townsmen resented his rise in social class. Burke now manoeuvred for Crabbe to be made chaplain to the Duke of Rutland at Belvoir Castle in Leicestershire.

The Duke and Duchess, were kind and generous to him as were their friends who enjoyed his literary works. But his relationship with the others in the household was tense. With the publication in May 1783 of his poem The Village, Crabbe achieved popularity with both the public and critics. Samuel Johnson said of it in a letter to Reynolds "I have sent you back Mr. Crabbe's poem, which I read with great delight. It is original, vigorous, and elegant."

It was decided that, as Chaplain to a noble family, Crabbe was in need of a college degree, and his name was entered on the boards of Trinity College, Cambridge, and through various influences Crabbe obtained a degree without residence. This was 1783, but almost immediately he received an LL.B. degree from the Archbishop of Canterbury. This allowed Crabbe to be given two small livings in Dorsetshire, Frome St Quintin and Evershot.

On the strength of these preferments and a promise of future assistance from the Duke, Crabbe and Sarah Elmy were married in December 1783, in the parish church of Beccles.

In 1784 the Duke of Rutland became Lord Lieutenant of Ireland. It was agreed that Crabbe would not go to Ireland, though the two men parted as close friends. The newly-weds stayed on at Belvoir for another eighteen months before Crabbe accepted a vacant curacy in Stathern in Leicestershire, moving there in 1785. The couple had four children of which only two sons survived; George (1785) and John (1787).

In October 1787, at age 35, the Duke of Rutland died in Dublin, after a short illness. The Duchess, anxious to have their former chaplain close by, was able to get Crabbe the two livings of Muston, Leicestershire, and Allington, Lincolnshire, in exchange for his old livings. Crabbe brought his family to Muston in February 1789.

Crabbe was also a coleopterist and recorder of beetles, and is credited for discovering the first specimen of Calosoma sycophanta L. to be recorded from Suffolk. He published an essay, in 1790, on the Natural History of the Vale of Belvoir. It includes over 70 species of local coleopterans.

In 1792, through the death of one of Sarah's relations and her older sister, the Crabbe family came into possession of an estate in Parham, which, at a stroke, removed all of their financial worries. Crabbe soon moved his family to the inheritance.

Crabbe's life at Parham was not happy. The former owner of the estate had been popular for his hospitality, while Crabbe's lifestyle was much more private. His solace here was the company of his friend Dudley Long North and his fellow Whigs who lived nearby.

After four years at Parham, the Crabbes moved to a home in Great Glemham, Suffolk, placed at his disposal by Dudley North.

In 1796 their third son, Edmund, died at the age of six. The death shredded Sarah's mental health and she never recovered. Crabbe, a devoted husband, tended her until her death many years later.

During his time at Glemham, Crabbe composed several novels, none of which were published. After Glemham, Crabbe moved to the village of Rendham in Suffolk, where he stayed until 1805. His poem The Parish Register was all but completed whilst here, and The Borough was also begun.

In September 1807, Crabbe published a new volume of poems which included The Library, The Newspaper, The Village and The Parish Register, to which were added Sir Eustace Grey and The Hall of Justice. It has been decades since his last publication but now, with this, he was seen as an important poet. Four editions were issued in 18 months. The reviews were unanimous in approval, headed by Francis Jeffrey in the critically important Edinburgh Review.

In 1809 Crabbe sent a copy of his poems to Walter Scott, who, in reply told Crabbe "how for more than twenty years he had desired the pleasure of a personal introduction to him, and how, as a lad of eighteen, he had met with selections from The Village and The Library in The Annual Register." This exchange of letters led to a friendship that lasted for the rest of their lives.

The success of The Parish Register encouraged Crabbe to proceed with a far longer poem, which he had been working on for several years. The Borough was begun at Rendham in Suffolk in 1801, continued at Muston after his return in 1805, and finally completed during a long visit to Aldeburgh in the autumn of 1809. It was published in 1810. In spite of its defects, The Borough was an outright success and went through six editions in the next six years. (Benjamin Britten's opera Peter Grimes is based on The Borough).

The following three years were especially lonely for him. His two sons, George and John, and were now clergymen themselves, each holding a local curacy enabling them to live under the parental roof, but Sarah's health was very poor, and Crabbe had no-one to help him with her care for most of the time.

Crabbe's next volume of poetry, Tales was published in the summer of 1812. It received a warm welcome from the poet's admirers, and was again warmly reviewed by Jeffrey in the Edinburgh Review. It is now considered Crabbe's masterpiece.

In the summer of 1813, Sarah felt well enough to visit London again. Crabbe, Sarah and their two sons spent nearly three months there. Crabbe was able to visit Dudley North and some of his other old friends, and to visit and help the poor and distressed, remembering his own want and misery in the great city thirty years earlier. The family returned to Muston in September, and at October's end Sarah died at the age of 63. Within days of her death Crabbe fell seriously ill. He rallied, however, and returned to the duties of his parish.

In 1814, he became Rector of Trowbridge in Wiltshire, a position given to him by the new Duke of Rutland. He now remained at Trowbridge for the rest of his life.

His two sons followed him, as soon as their existing engagements allowed them to leave Leicestershire. The younger son, John, became his father's curate, and the elder, became curate at Pucklechurch, also nearby. Crabbe's reputation as a poet continued to grow in these years. This made him a welcome guest in many houses. Nearby was the poet William Lisle Bowles, who introduced Crabbe to the noble family at Bowood House, home of the Marquess of Lansdowne, who was always ready to welcome those distinguished in literature and the arts. It was at Bowood House that Crabbe first met the poet Samuel Rogers, who became a close friend and had an influence on Crabbe's poetry. In 1817, on the advice of Rogers, Crabbe stayed in London in the early summer to enjoy the literary society of the capital. Here he met Thomas Campbell, and through him and Rogers was introduced to his future publisher John Murray.

In June 1819, Crabbe published his collection Tales of the Hall.

Around 1820 Crabbe began suffering from frequent severe attacks of neuralgia, and this, together with his advancing years, made him less and less able to travel to London.

In the spring of 1822, Crabbe met Walter Scott for the first time in London, and promised to visit him in Scotland in the fall. He kept this promise during George IV's visit to Edinburgh.

Later in 1822, Crabbe was invited to spend Christmas at Belvoir Castle, but weather made the trip impossible. While at home, he continued to write a large amount of poetry (eventually leaving 21 manuscript volumes at his death).

Crabbe continued to visit at Hampstead throughout the 1820s, often meeting the writer Joanna Baillie and her sister Agnes.

In November 1832 he went to see his son George, at Pucklechurch. He was able to preach twice for his son, who congratulated him on the power of his voice, and other encouraging signs of strength. "I will venture a good sum, sir," he said, "that you will be assisting me ten years hence." "Ten weeks" was Crabbe's answer, and the prediction proved eerily accurate. Crabbe now returned to Trowbridge.

Early in January of the New Year he reported more drowsiness and increasing weakness. Later in the month he was laid low by a severe cold. Further complications arose, and it soon became apparent that he would not live much longer.

George Crabbe died on February 3rd, 1832, aged 77 at Trowbridge, Wiltshire with his two sons by his side.

George Crabbe – A Concise Bibliography

Sketch of Crabbe (1826)
Inebriety (1775)
The Candidate (1780)
The Library (1781)
The Village (1782)
The Newspaper (1785)
Poems (1807)

The Borough (1810)
Tales in Verse (1812)
Tales of the Hall (1819)
Posthumous Tales (1834)